KU-632-192

MCQs for the MRCOG Part II

by **Patrick Hogston**
BSc, FRCS, MRCOG

Consultant Obstetrician and Gynaecologist,
Department of Obstetrics and Gynaecology,
St Mary's Hospital, Portsmouth, PO3 6AD

KLUWER ACADEMIC PUBLISHERS
BOSTON / DORDRECHT / LONDON

Petroc Press, an imprint of Librapharm Limited

Acknowledgements

Thanks to Carrie for typing and encouragement

Distributors

Plymbridge Distributors Limited, Plymbridge House, Estover Road, Plymouth, PL6 7PZ UK

Copyright

©1995 Kluwer Academic Publishers
©1996 Librapharm Limited
Reprinted 1996 under the Petroc Press imprint

All rights reserved. No part of this publication may be reproduced, stored in a retrieval system, or transmitted in any form or by any means, electronic, mechanical, photocopying, recording or otherwise, without prior permission from the publishers.

Whilst every attempt has been made to ensure that the information provided in this book is correct at the time of printing, the publisher, its distributors and agents, make no representation, express or otherwise, with regard to the accurac of the information contained herein and cannot accept any legal responsibility or liability for any errors or omissions that may have been made or for any loss or damage resulting from the use of the information.

Published in the United Kingdom by Librapharm Limited ,Gemini House, 162 Craven Road, Newbury, Berkshire, UK, RG14 5NR

A catalogue record for this book is available from the British Library .

ISBN 1- 900603-55-1

Printed and bound in the United Kingdom by Hartnolls Limited, Bodmin, Cornwall

# Contents

P/O NO:
ACCESSION NO: KHO3213
SHELFMARK: ~~LIB/HDC~~

616.0076/HOG

Introduction

This book of MCQ questions is a revision aid for MRCOG candidates. For this reason some questions may be controversial, something that is avoided in the real examination. However in order to stimulate thought and further reading I felt it would be helpful to include a few such questions and hope the candidate finds this useful. In the MRCOG questions one hour is allowed to answer 25 questions and you should therefore practise against the clock. MCQ examinations are familiar to most doctors but undoubtedly repeated practice improves performance. I hope therefore that this book will help successful preparation for the Part II MRCOG.

Patrick Hogston

Questions

Blood pressure in pregnancy:

A Is exclusively determined by total peripheral resistance and cardiac output

B Rises in response to angiotensin from 10 weeks

C Should be measured using a large cuff if the upper arm circumference is greater than 35 cm

D Will be artificially lowered if taken in the right arm with the patient on her left side

E A reading of 140/90 mmHg in the third trimester readily identifies hypertensive women

The following conditions can be excluded by high resolution ultrasound at 20 weeks of pregnancy:

A Holoprosencephaly

B Gastroschisis

C Cystic fibrosis

D Infantile polycystic kidneys

E Hypoplastic left heart

3 **A pregnant woman with asthma:**

A Should not be treated with aminophylline

B Can be safely treated with steroids in status asthmaticus

C Bronchospasm can be a presenting symptom of pulmonary embolism

D Has at least twice the chance of having a child who will develop asthma than does a non-asthmatic woman

E Cannot be induced with prostaglandin E_2 pessaries

4 **Thromboembolic disease in pregnancy:**

A Is the commonest cause of maternal death

B Has a 20% recurrence risk in pregnancy

C Venography and isotope lung scanning must not be used

D Treatment with subcutaneous heparin may cause thrombocytopenia

E One third of deaths from pulmonary embolism occur antenatally

5 **In pregnancy:**

A A haemoglobin of 11 g/dl is the lower limit of normal according to WHO guidelines

B A low serum iron with a low total iron binding capacity suggests iron deficiency

C The overall total iron requirement is approximately 1000 mg

D Iron absorption from the jejunum is increased

E Iron should be advised for all women

6 **The following statements about the neonate are true:**

A An Apgar score of 3 at 5 minutes predicts a 50% chance of subsequent cerebral palsy

B Continuous electronic fetal heart rate monitoring in labour reduces the chance of neonatal seizures

C Poor feeding and jaundice may be the only signs of neonatal septicaemia

D The commonest cause of death in the first year of life is the sudden infant death syndrome (SIDS)

E Sensineural deafness is a recognised complication of perinatal hypoxia

7 **The following conditions have an autosomal dominant mode of inheritance:**

A Achondroplasia

B Phenylketonuria

C Tuberous sclerosis

D Huntington's chorea

E Friedreich's ataxia

8 **Shoulder dystocia is closely associated with:**

A An estimated fetal weight of 4 kg on ultrasound

B Rotational forceps delivery

C Anencephaly

D 42 week gestation

E Oxytocin augmentation for primary dysfunctional labour

9 Which of the following increase the risk of a Caesarean section in a primigravida at 41 weeks gestation?

A Fresh meconium liquor seen in labour

B Booking for consultant unit delivery

C Continuous electronic fetal monitoring with fetal blood sampling

D Oxytocin augmentation for secondary arrest at 8 cm

E Maternal height of 145 cm

10 Primary postpartum haemorrhage (PPH):

A Is best prevented by ergometrine alone in routine practice

B Is due to trauma to the genital tract in 10% of cases

C Is more common in women with myotonic dystrophy

D Is related to fetal weight

E When the cause of maternal death, is often due to delay in performing hysterectomy

11 Ectopic pregnancy:

A Has a higher incidence in women with copper intrauterine contraceptive devices (IUDs) than in women not using contraception

B Is excluded by the presence of an intrauterine gestational sac on ultrasound

C Is best treated by laparoscopic salpingostomy

D Is excluded by a negative serum β-HCG

E Has a recurrence rate of 15% after conservative surgery

12 **The combined oral contraceptive pill:**

A Is relatively safe to continue up to the age of 40 in a woman who does not smoke

B Alters glucose tolerance

C Increases the incidence of vaginal candidiasis

D May be used as a means of post-coital contraception

E Increases the risk of ovarian cancer

13 **Babies born with intrauterine growth retardation:**

A Are best diagnosed by centile weight charts

B Usually exhibit catch up growth during infancy

C Have 20% risk of speech, language and learning difficulties

D Have a risk of pulmonary haemorrhage

E Have a risk of pneumothorax

14 **Hyperstimulation syndrome of the ovary:**

A Can occur with clomiphene

B Is worse in conception cycles

C Occurs in at least one third of IVF/GIFT cycles

D Can present with respiratory failure

E Laparotomy is useful to drain the cysts

15 Concerning polycystic ovary syndrome:

[A] Most women are obese

[B] Is familial

[C] Fertility is reduced by the oral contraceptive pill

[D] Is characterised by a thick walled capsule and a normal number of primary and secondary follicles

[E] Is excluded by a normal serum luteinising hormone level

16 The most significant prognostic factor in cervical carcinoma is:

[A] Histological type

[B] Tumour volume

[C] Resection margins at surgery

[D] Smoking

[E] Age

17 In advanced cervical cancer:

[A] Renal impairment secondary to ureteric obstruction will alter the excretion of many cytotoxic drugs used

[B] Prior surgery alters the pattern of disease recurrence and makes distant metastases more likely

[C] Prior radiotherapy alters the blood supply to structures and makes delivery of adequate amounts of cytotoxic drug to areas of recurrence within the irradiated field more difficult

[D] Platinum can achieve 50% response rates

[E] Exenterative surgery no longer has a place

18 Cone biopsy of the cervix:

A Reduces fertility

B Should be avoided in pregnancy

C Is adequate treatment for microcarcinoma Stage 1a1

D Requires a general anaesthetic

E Is diagnostic if the smear shows glandular abnormalities

19 Optimum treatment of a 30-year-old woman with 3 cm adenocarcinoma of the cervix includes:

A Radical hysterectomy and pelvic lymphadenectomy

B Para-aortic lymphadenectomy

C Bilateral salpingo-oophorectomy if surgery is undertaken

D Neoadjuvant cisplatinum

E Post-operative radiotherapy

20 Borderline tumours of the ovary:

A Are benign in nature

B Chemotherapy is required for extra-ovarian implants

C Conservative surgery is appropriate if childbearing is not complete

D After total abdominal hysterectomy and bilateral salpingo-oophorectomy, hormone replacement therapy should be avoided

E Ploidy correlates well with prognosis

21 **The following are associated with an increased survival in advanced cancer of the ovary:**

A Cytoreductive debulking surgery

B Cisplatinum

C Hormone replacement therapy

D Logarithmic fall in serum Ca125 during chemotherapy

E Second look laparotomy after completion of chemotherapy with second line chemotherapy if positive

22 **The following are true of gestational trophoblastic tumours:**

A Anatomical site of disease is the most important determinant of outcome

B Outlook is worse after a spontaneous miscarriage than a term pregnancy

C Infection is the commonest cause of death

D Partial moles are triploid

E Etoposide is useful in patients who relapse

23 **Concerning endometrial cancer:**

A Prognosis is worse if the adjacent endometrium is atrophic

B Staging requires measurement of the depth of invasion of the myometrium

C Is commoner in women with polycystic ovary disease

D The prognosis is worsened by post-operative hormone replacement therapy

E Vault recurrence is better prevented by vault irradiation pre operatively than post-operatively

24 Vulvar carcinoma:

A One positive Cloquet's node requires pelvic lymphadenectomy

B Spreads by embolisation

C A lesion of 5 mm depth requires wide local excision only

D One positive inguinal node is an indication for pelvic radiotherapy

E The depth of invasion is easily measured by the pathologist

25 In a normal pregnancy:

A Arterial pCO_2 levels rise

B Renal blood flow increases by 50%

C Serum alkaline phosphatase rises

D Serum LH rises

E Serum aldosterone rises

26 4th degree tears of the perineum (involvement of anal mucosa):

A Are prevented by episiotomy

B Can be repaired under local anaesthetic

C Result in an incomplete anatomical sphincter at 3 months in at least 30% of women

D Is less common after ventouse than forceps delivery

E A rectovaginal fistula may still occur even with expert repair

27 **Vomiting in pregnancy:**

A Is most commonly due to pyelonephritis

B May be due to appendicitis

C Steroids are useful in intractable cases

D Does not occur with ectopic pregnancies

E May lead to a Mallory Weiss tear

28 **A woman with ruptured membranes at 29 weeks gestation:**

A Should be started on antibiotics

B Should not be given steroids as the greatest risk to the fetus is infection

C May have a prolapsed cord

D If Group B streptococcus is cultured from the vagina treatment should be maintained during labour until delivery

E Should be delivered by Caesarean section if she develops a fever and fetal tachycardia

29 **The following conditions of the fetus are associated with at least a 10% risk of a chromosomal abnormality:**

A Bilateral choroid plexus cysts

B Dilated renal pelvis

C Gastroschisis

D Omphalocoele

E Cystic hygroma

30 The following conditions tend to improve with pregnancy:

A Migraine

B Rheumatoid arthritis

C Multiple sclerosis

D Asthma

E Epilepsy

31 Pre-eclampsia is associated with:

A A lack of trophoblastic infiltration of arterial walls

B Acute arterial atherosis

C Decreased arterial sensitivity to angiotensin II

D Glomerular endotheliosis

E Increased circulating volume

32 Pre-eclampsia:

A Is commoner in smokers

B Is most likely inherited as a single recessive gene

C Is commoner in monozygotic than dizygotic twins

D Progresses to eclampsia less often when antihypertensive therapy is used

E Requires anticonvulsant therapy with phenytoin in severe cases

33 **Severe pre-eclampsia can result in:**

A Blindness

B Microangiopathic haemolysis

C Low cardiac output

D Thrombocytopenia

E Liver failure

34 **Low dose aspirin in pregnancy:**

A Was given at a dose of 75 mg daily in the CLASP study

B Increases the risk of antepartum haemorrhage

C Increases the risk of blood transfusion post delivery

D Reduces the risk of perinatal death due to intrauterine growth retardation

E Is only of benefit to women with previous pre-eclampsia before 32 weeks

35 **Breech presentations:**

A External cephalic version (ECV) reduces the risk of Caesarean section

B ECV can take place in the antenatal clinic

C ECV cannot be performed once labour has started

D If ECV fails Caesarean section should be offered to all women

E Should be screened for a fetal abnormality

36 Women complaining of menorrhagia:

A Cannot be losing more than 80 ml of blood per month if their haemoglobin is 13 g/dl

B Menstrual flow is reliably estimated by the number of towels or tampons used

C Cyklokapron reduces menstrual flow by a non-specific action on the endometrium

D Cyklokapron reduces menstrual blood flow by 50% in women losing > 80 ml/month

E Cyklokapron can only be prescribed for 3 months

37 Urinary tract infection:

A Should be prevented in women with an indwelling catheter by the prescription of antibiotics

B With an indwelling catheter, a urine culture of > 100 000 *E. coli* is better treated by removal of the catheter than by antibiotics

C Intermittent clean self-catheterisation results in less morbidity than supra-pubic catheterisation

D Post-operative catheterisation is obligatory after vaginal hysterectomy for menorrhagia

E The presence of lactobacilli is treated with ampicillin

GENERAL HOSPITAL
KERRY
618 Hogs
LIBRARY
KGH
1410

38   Hirsutism:

A May be treated by dexamethasone when there is an adrenal cause

B Cyproterone acetate results in reduction of libido

C Treatment cannot be assessed before six months

D 99% of circulating testosterones are protein bound

E Raised dehydroepiandosterone levels confirm polycystic ovary syndrome

39   Endometriosis:

A Is associated with unruptured luteinised follicle

B Severity of disease is determined by the American Fertility Score

C Can be treated with 200 mg danazol daily

D Results of medical treatment are poor compared to surgery

E Cannot occur de novo after sterilisation

40   A 14-year-old girl with menorrhagia and a haemoglobin of 8 g:

A Requires diagnostic curettage

B Will have a clotting disorder in 10% of cases

C Is best treated with the combined contraceptive pill

D Is more likely to have a hysterectomy than a girl without adolescent menorrhagia

E Is due to increased prostaglandin production by the endometrium

41 Spontaneous rupture of the membranes at term:

[A] Results in a higher rate of Caesarean section if induction of labour is performed than awaiting spontaneous labour

[B] Induction of labour increases rate of infection over awaiting spontaneous labour

[C] Induction of labour reduces the risk to the fetus

[D] Results in spontaneous labour in 90% within 48 hours

[E] Diagnosis by nitrazene swabs has 15% false positive rate

42 Women with a history of prior delivery by Caesarean section:

[A] Should have X-ray pelvimetry before deciding mode of delivery

[B] Should not labour if they have had two previous lower segment operations

[C] Should have the uterus explored digitally after a vaginal delivery

[D] Should not have trial labour if previous Caesarean section was followed by infection

[E] Can deliver a bigger baby vaginally if the previous operation was for dystocia

43 The following procedures will effectively treat a cystocoele:

[A] Colposuspension

[B] Stamey endoscopic bladder neck suspension

[C] Sacral colpopexy

[D] Insertion of a shelf pessary

[E] Aldridge sling

44 **Intermittent clean self-catheterisation can play an important role in the long-term post-operative management of the following operations:**

A Radical hysterectomy

B Colposuspension

C Anterior repair with buttressing of urethra

D Stamey endoscopic bladder neck suspension

E Sacrospinous colpopexy

45 **At the menopause:**

A 25% of women suffer no vasomotor symptoms

B Norethisterone has been shown to relieve hot flushes in placebo studies ✓

C 5 years of oestrogen therapy reduces risk of hip fracture by 50%

D Hormone replacement therapy (HRT) may be associated with weight gain

E HRT is contraindicated by a history of deep vein thrombosis on the oral contraceptive pill

46 Hormone replacement therapy for postmenopausal women:

[A] Should be stopped four weeks prior to major surgery

[B] Norethisterone reduces HDL-cholesterol

[C] Ethinyl oestradiol is more potent than conjugated equine oestrogens

[D] Serum levels of oestradiol are half the premenopausal range

[E] Intolerance to progestagens may be reduced by continuous use of 1 mg norethisterone

47 Intrauterine contraceptive devices:

[A] Should be removed as soon as possible if pregnancy is confirmed

[B] With lost threads are better investigated by X-ray than ultrasound

[C] The use of general anaesthesia increases risk of perforation

[D] Should be removed if *Actinomyces* is found on a routine smear

[E] Duration of use increases the risk of subfertility

48 A couple complain of inability to conceive after two years of unprotected intercourse:

[A] Treatment for low sperm counts is intrauterine insemination

[B] 95% of pregnancies will occur in this time

[C] Varicocoele should be sought and treated surgically

[D] In unexplained infertility age is the most important prognostic factor

[E] Azoospermia due to congenital occlusion of the vas can be treated surgically

49 Spontaneous abortion at 8 weeks:

A Is uncommon once a live fetus has been seen on ultrasound

B Is often due to chromosomal abnormalities in the conceptus

C Can often be prevented by injection of HCG

D May lead to acute pelvic infection

E May be caused by hepatitis

50 The menopause:

A The average age in the UK is 55 years

B Is earlier in smokers

C Plasma cholesterol and triglyceride levels fall

D If below 40 requires ovarian biopsy for confirmation

E May be influenced by vaginal hysterectomy

51 Antenatal care should include:

A Serial vaginal examinations if previous preterm labour

B Anti-D immunoglobulin at 28 weeks for Rhesus negative women

C A consultation with an obstetrician

D Mothers carrying their own notes

E Screening all women for hepatitis B

52 **Improvement in perinatal mortality figures could be achieved by:**

A Routine use of kick charts

B Routine screening by Doppler ultrasound at 18 weeks

C Preventing preterm birth

D Increase in Caesarean section rate

E Induction of labour at term plus 8 days

53 **Human immunodeficiency virus (HIV) infection:**

A HIV virus is an RNA retrovirus

B Is inevitably passed from mother to fetus

C Causes an increased risk of cervical intraepithelial neoplasia

D Results in a fall in CD4 lymphocyte count in pregnant women

E Is a contraindication to breastfeeding

54 **The oral contraceptive pill protects against:**

A Breast cancer

B Ovarian cancer

C Endometriosis

D Pelvic inflammatory disease

E Cervical intraepithelial neoplasia

55 **The following are more common in the female child:**

[A] Talipes equino-varus

[B] Congenital dislocation of the hip

[C] Isolated cleft palate

[D] Pyloric stenosis

[E] Hirschsprung's disease

56 **The premenstrual syndrome:**

[A] May be confused with manic depressive illness

[B] Is confirmed in less than 50% by prospective symptom charts

[C] Will be helped by hysterectomy

[D] Is associated with reduced β-endorphin levels

[E] May indicate the climacteric

57 **Depoprovera (medroxyprogesterone acetate):**

[A] Suppresses pituitary gonadotrophins

[B] Effect may last for one year after last injection

[C] Reduces HDL levels

[D] Should not be used for diabetics

[E] Is contraindicated in hypertensive women

58 Chorionic villus biopsy:

[A] Is indicated for maternal age of 39

[B] May cause limb deformities

[C] Has a similar miscarriage rate to amniocentesis

[D] May diagnose cystic fibrosis

[E] Has a risk that is operator dependent

59 A woman with a raised alphafetoprotein (AFP) at 16 weeks:

[A] Her risk of a neural tube defect (NTD) is independent of the local prevalence rate

[B] Should have test repeated urgently

[C] Has an increased risk of low birthweight baby

[D] Is less likely to be Afro-Caribbean

[E] Has a higher risk of a NTD if a diabetic

60 Acute pelvic inflammatory disease (PID):

[A] May be treated with azithromycin

[B] Is excluded by a positive pregnancy test

[C] Results in infertility in 5% after one episode

[D] Is associated with retention of urine

[E] Requires laparoscopy for confirmation

61 Breastfeeding:

A Is contraindicated with maternal warfarin therapy

B Prevents ovulation for 3 months

C Should be stopped if mastitis occurs

- D Is enhanced by antenatal nipple care

E Requires high fluid intake

62 Gestational diabetes mellitus:

A Should be screened for in all pregnancies

6 B May be excluded by a fasting glucose

C Oral glucose tolerance test is reliably reproducible

D Is an indication for induction at 38 weeks

E Is a precursor of diabetes in later life

63 Urge incontinence:

A May be a symptom of multiple sclerosis

B Drug treatment is limited by side-effects

C May be due to prolapse

D Cystoscopy is indicated

E Clam cystoplasty is indicated only in sensory urgency

64 Urodynamic testing:

A Is painful in sensory disorders

B Urethral pressure profile required before surgery for urethral sphincter incompetence

C In detrusor instability shows pressure rise during filling

D Cannot assess bladder capacity accurately

E Can be performed by a nurse

65 Urinary flow rate:

A Is high in stress incontinence

B Is high in detrusor instability

C Requires 200 ml of urine for an accurate result

D Must be measured before colposuspension

E May be affected by eversion of vagina

66 Bleeding at 4 weeks post delivery:

A Requires a cervical smear

B May be normal

C Requires curettage

D Risk of choriocarcinoma is 1%

E Can be treated by the oral contraceptive pill

67 *Candida albicans:*

A May be asymptomatic

B Is commoner on the oral contraceptive pill

C Occurs in partners of infected women

D Commonly occurs before menstruation

E Is carried in gastrointestinal tract

68 Recurrent *Candida* infection:

A May be due to drug resistance

B May be due to non-*albicans* strains

C Irritation may be due to local treatment

D Monthly fluconazole is better than daily ketoconazole

E May be excluded by negative microscopy

69 A pregnant woman with a history of recurrent genital herpes:

A Should be assessed early in labour for lesions

B Should have weekly cultures of the cervix from 36 weeks

C Should have a Caesarean section if she presents with spontaneous rupture of the membranes

D Should have acyclovir prophylaxis

E 50% of neonatal infections give no maternal history

70 **Genital warts at 12 weeks pregnancy may be treated by:**

A Carbon dioxide laser

B Podophyllin

C Trichloroacetic acid

D Observation

E 5-Fluoruracil

71 **Toxoplasmosis:** ✓

A Is more commonly acquired by the fetus if the mother is infected in the first trimester

B Leads to serious fetal effects in 50% of transmissions

C Spiromycin is an effective treatment in the third trimester

D Is a cause of neonatal seizures

E Reduction in the number of affected neonates would be better achieved by health education than by screening in the UK

72 **Acute retention of urine in women may be due to:**

A Preoperative anxiety

B Vulval herpes

C Multiple sclerosis

D Radical hysterectomy

E Retroverted uterus in pregnancy

73 Urinary tract infection in pregnancy:

A Is prevented by screening at booking

B Should be treated with intravenous antibiotics if fever is present

C Antibiotics should be continued as a prophylactic measure after first attack

D Is associated with preterm delivery

E Can be treated with a single dose of 3 g ampicillin

74 The following organisms can be detected on a cervical smear:

A *Candida albicans*

B *Actinomyces israeli*

C Herpes simplex

D *Trichomonas vaginalis*

E Human papilloma virus (HPV)

75 Cystic fibrosis:

A Gene frequency is 1:50

B Incidence 1:5000 live births

C Carriers can be identified by a mouth wash

D Is diagnosed in neonatal period by raised serum immunoreactive trypsin

E Involves impaired humoral immunity

76 A pregnancy of term plus 10 days:

A Requires antenatal surveillance by biophysical testing

B Induction of labour reduces the risk of perinatal death

C Increased risk of congenital malformation

D Is due to postmaturity

E Increased risk of intrapartum asphyxia

77 Preterm babies weighing less than 1500 g:

A Require routine intubation at birth

B Surfactant reduces risk of periventricular haemorrhage

C Surfactant reduces risk of pneumothorax

D Require vitamin K

E Should be given sodium bicarbonate

78 Ultrasound in obstetric practice:

A Routine use reduces incidence of induction for post dates

B Doppler reduces perinatal deaths in high risk pregnancies

C Is an essential part of triple screening for Down's syndrome

D Has been shown safe in controlled trials

E Does not have a false positive rate for congenital malformations

79 GnRH analogues:

[A] Have only an inhibitory effect on pituitary gonadotrophins

[B] Are useful long term treatment for fibroids

[C] Produce menopausal hormone profile

[D] Cause osteoporosis

[E] Should not be used in young women

80 Transverse lie:

[A] Is a non-recurrent condition

[B] Will persist after 37 weeks

[C] Labour should be induced if it reverts to cephalic after 37 weeks

[D] At Caesarean section is managed by internal version after incising the lower segment

[E] If it leads to difficulty in delivery after a lower segment incision this should be extended in the midline as an inverted T incision

81 The following risks apply to drug administration in first trimester of pregnancy:

[A] Sodium valproate and neural tube defects

[B] Tetracycline and dental discoloration

[C] Metronidazole and skeletal abnormalities

[D] Azathioprine and cranio-facial abnormalities

[E] Isoniazid and 8th cranial nerve damage

82 The following drugs taken by lactating mothers may have clinically detectable effects on newborn:

A Amiodarone

B Sulphasalazine

C Carbamazepine

D Carbimazole

E Metronidazole

83 Enterocoele:

A Always accompanies procidentia

B Is best demonstrated by dynamic proctography

C At abdominal surgery is treated by Halban's technique

D Is best prevented by McCall's culdoplasty at vaginal hysterectomy for prolapse

E Is always posterior to the vaginal vault

84 Concerning the management of an abnormal smear:

A Squamous metaplasia is easily distinguished from cervical intraepithelial neoplasia (CIN) at colposcopy

B At colposcopy the intensity of staining with acetic acid is a useful guide to the severity of the lesion

C Destructive therapy has been replaced by large loop excision of the transformation zone

D CIN may regress

E Six weeks should elapse between cone biopsy and radical hysterectomy because of the risk of infection

85 Group B streptococcal infection:

A Causes serious effects in 30% of colonised babies

B Prophylactic penicillin to neonates leads to higher mortality

C Maternal treatment reduces neonatal morbidity only if continued throughout labour

D Is commoner in infants weighing less than 2500 g

E A rapid diagnostic screening test for preterm labour would help reduce neonatal morbidity

86 Maternal sickle cell syndrome:

A Includes haemoglobin SC disease

B Increases pregnancy loss due to preterm birth

C Repeated blood transfusion leads to presence of atypical red cell antibodies

D Regional anaesthesia may predispose to sickling

E Is associated with dehydration in labour

87 Anorexia nervosa:

A Causes breast atrophy

B Has a mortality of 15%

C Serum gonadotrophin levels are raised

D Fertility remains depressed even if normal menses return

E Is recurrent

88 **Post-natal depression:**

[A] Affects 10% of women after discharge home

[B] Recurrence rate reduced if pregnancy delayed for two years

[C] Oestrogen therapy is useful

[D] When required hospital admission is usually for a minimum of six weeks

[E] There is a risk of suicide and infanticide

89 **Female athletes are often amenorrhoeic:**

[A] They are therefore at risk of osteoporosis

[B] Menstruation depends on the amount of body fat

[C] Should have serum FSH measured

[D] Have reduced fertility in later life

[E] Should avoid the oral contraceptive pill

90 **A 70-year-old woman complains of pruritis vulvae. A vulval biopsy shows lichen sclerosus:**

[A] Lichen sclerosus is a premalignant condition

[B] Is best treated with low dose steroid cream

[C] Simple vulvectomy is a good long term treatment

[D] Usually respond to oestrogen cream

[E] Antihistamines are not helpful in management

91 Clomiphene citrate:

A Blocks oestrogen receptors in the hypothalamus

B Causes hot flushes

C If pregnancy does not occur within six months other causes should be considered

D Has an adverse effect on cervical mucus

E Is not associated with multiple pregnancy

92 A pregnant woman is suspected of having thyrotoxicosis. The following statements are true:

A Urinary excretion of iodide falls

B Fetal TSH is higher than the mother at term

C Family history will be irrelevant

D Thyroid stimulating immunoglobulin will not be present in women previously treated for thyrotoxicosis

E If confirmed, surgery is the best treatment

93 Pregnant women with renal transplants:

A Show a fall in creatinine clearance by up to 15% in the third trimester

B Should have the dose of immunosuppressants increased

C Should be prescribed prophylactic antibiotics against urinary infection

D Have an increased risk of preterm delivery

E May have pelvic osteodystrophy

94   Concerning osteoporosis:

A Biochemical composition of osteoporotic bone is altered

B Hip fractures occupy 10% of orthopaedic beds in the UK

C 15% of bone mass is lost in the first 10 years of menopause

D Etidronate reduces vertebral fracture rates

E Estrogen does not result in gain in bone density

95   Investigations for primary amenorrhoea include:

A Skull X-ray

B Pelvic ultrasound

C Chromosome analysis

D Serum oestradiol

E Serum prolactin

96   Oral progesterone-only contraception:

A Is contraindicated in porphyria

B May cause depression

C Is contraindicated by valvular heart disease

D Inhibits ovulation

E Can be used by migraine sufferers

97 Precocious puberty:

A Is usually constitutional

B Is associated with long bone fractures

C Pubic hair is first sign

D Can be halted by GnRH analogues

E Results in short stature

98 Childhood vulvovaginitis may be treated by:

A Mebendazole

B Erythromycin

C Attention to hygiene

D Oestrogen cream

E Clotrimazole

99 A 40-year-old woman with advanced carcinoma of the cervix is admitted confused and in pain:

A Hypercalcaemia may be the cause of her confusion

B Transcutaneous nerve stimulation is useful for pain

C A percutaneous cervical cordotomy is useful for unilateral sciatic nerve pain

D Opiates are the commonest cause of confusion in terminal care of cancer of the cervix

E Co-danthremer should be used prophylactically for constipation

100 A woman presents with advanced recurrent carcinoma of the ovary 2 years after the initial treatment. The following statements are correct:

A Surgery is useful for intestinal obstruction

B Response to chemotherapy will be poor

C A shunt is useful for ascites

D Haloperidol is a useful drug at night

E Cyclizine can be mixed with diamorphine in a syringe pump

101 Prostaglandins:

A Are produced by all cells

B The effect of prostaglandin E on the myometrium is different in the pregnant from the non-pregnant

C Are metabolised in the liver

D Are involved in ovulation

E Prostacyclin inhibits platelet aggregation

102 Risk factors for osteoporosis include:

A Family history

B Smoking

C Afro-Caribbean origin

D Caffeine

E Hypothyroidism

103 Pregnant diabetic women:

A Should avoid pregnancy if retinopathy is present

B Serum fructosamine is a measure of recent control

C Should have very tight control of their disease

D Induced at 38 weeks

E Have children whose risk of developing disease is 5%

104 The following associations apply in pregnancy:

A Smoking and preterm delivery

B Use of VDUs and congenital heart malformations

C Fetal alcohol syndrome and hydrocephaly

D Pyrimethamine and teratogenesis

E Phenytoin and cleft palate

105 Screening for breast cancer:

A Is offered to women over 60

B Is offered at three-yearly intervals

C Is present in 2% of women at their first visit

D Involves 1 million women per year

E Prevents 8% of deaths

106 Acute ulcerative colitis in pregnancy:

A Requires antibiotics

B Steroids should be withheld before 18 weeks

C May be confused with *Campylobacter* infection

D Requires barium enema for diagnosis

E Surgery is rarely required

107 Sudden infant death syndrome:

A Is the commonest cause of death in the first year of life after the perinatal period

B Is more likely in a sibling of a twin who has died of it

C Is more likely in Asian infants

D Is reduced by sleeping the infant prone

E Is unrelated to parental smoking

108 The vaginal contraceptive diaphragm:

A Should be left in the vagina for 6 h

B Should be replaced yearly

C Reduces the incidence of chlamydial infection

D Should be measured by digital vaginal examination

E Does not require refitting after an elective Caesarean section

109 The following potentiate the action of warfarin:

A Cimetidine

B Danazol

C Metronidazole

D Thyroxine

E Aspirin

110 The following are part of a normal bereavement reaction:

A A period of numbness

B Auditory hallucinations

C Visual hallucinations

D Searching behaviour

E Thought insertion

111 Contraception:

A Post-coital contraception should be completed within 72 hours

B An IUD can be inserted up to 5 days after unprotected intercourse for post-coital contraception

C Desogestrol is the least androgenic progestagen

D Antibiotic cover is required for insertion of an IUD in women who require antibiotics for dental treatment

E The oral contraceptive pill may stunt growth if used before 15 years

112 Osteoporosis can be caused by:

[A] Bed rest

[B] Heparin

[C] Thyrotoxicosis

[D] Frusemide

[E] Diabetes mellitus

113 Congenital malformations in babies of diabetic mothers:

[A] Cause half the perinatal deaths

[B] Are most often skeletal abnormalities

[C] Are commoner if control is poor in the first trimester

[D] Have fallen significantly in the last 30 years

[E] Are commoner in insulin-dependent than non-insulin-dependent mothers

114 A pregnant woman with a pulmonary embolism:

[A] Presents with pleural chest pain, haemoptysis and dyspnoea in 80% of cases

[B] Can be excluded by a normal ECG

[C] Requires a ventilation and perfusion scan for diagnosis

[D] May present as bronchospasm

[E] Should be screened for antithrombin III deficiency

115 Raised serum prolactin:

[A] Will be associated with galactorrhoea in most cases

[B] May be due to the venepuncture

[C] Hypothyroidism

[D] Head injury

[E] Chronic renal failure

116 A 25-year-old woman complains of six months of recurrent abdominal and pelvic pain:

[A] The most likely diagnosis is irritable bowel syndrome

[B] Should always undergo laparoscopy

[C] Dyspareunia increases the likelihood of endometriosis

[D] Should be screened for chlamydial infection

[E] May have menorrhagia and urinary symptoms

117 Bromocriptine for the treatment of hyperprolactinaemia:

[A] Nausea may affect compliance

[B] Causes hypotension

[C] May cause pleural effusions

[D] Is equally effective in acromegaly

[E] Can also be used for breast pain without identifiable cause (cyclical mastalgia)

118 Chronic pelvic pain after hysterectomy:

A Will not be due to a gynaecological cause if bilateral salpingo-oophorectomy was performed

B May be due to residual ovary syndrome

C Should be prescribed GnRH analogues before considering oophorectomy

D Surgery will involve ureteric dissection

E May be due to irritable bowel syndrome

119 Screening for ovarian cancer:

A Satisfies the WHO guidelines for screening

B Has been shown to reduce mortality from the disease

C Women with two affected first degree relatives should be offered prophylactic oophorectomy rather than screening

D Is more reliable with biochemical methods

E Ultrasound screening should be available in all district general hospitals

120 Fetal biophysical profile:

A Includes a cardiotocograph

B Reduces perinatal mortality in post dates pregnancies

C Fetal breathing stops before labour

D Fetal tone is useful

E Oligohydramnios predicts low Apgar score at birth

121 Trisomy 18:

A Is age related

B Only 10% survive the perinatal period

C Would be diagnosed on anomaly screening at 20 weeks

D Choroid plexus cysts are often present

E Commonly delivered by Caesarean section for fetal distress

122 Oophorectomy at the time of hysterectomy:

A Would prevent 8% of ovarian cancer if performed on all women over 40 years

B Can be performed laparoscopically at time of vaginal hysterectomy

C Mortality is increased by oophorectomy

D If not performed will lead to problems with pain in 5% of women

E May not prevent ovarian cancer in all women

123 The following tests may be useful in assessing male subfertility:

A Serum follicle stimulating hormone

B Cystoscopy

C Seminal fluid culture

D Testicular biopsy

E Testosterone

124 Mastalgia:

A Is associated with polycystic ovary syndrome

B Can be treated with bromocriptine

C Is worsened by oral contraceptive pill

D Is associated with breast cancer

E Is helped by danazol

125 A pregnant woman with varicella (chicken pox):

A Should receive zoster immunoglobulin

B Poses greatest risk to the child at delivery

C Should not use acyclovir

D Has an infection of little consequence to her

E Should not attend antenatal clinic

126 A primigravida is admitted at term with a painful antepartum haemorrhage and an absent fetal heart:

A Requires a blood transfusion

B Should have prostaglandin induction of labour

C Requires platelet transfusion

D Fibrin degradation products exacerbate the coagulation failure

E Is at risk of post-partum haemorrhage

127 The following are problems with artificial feeding:

A Jaundice

B Obesity

C Diarrhoea

D Vitamin K deficiency

E Tetany

128 A neonate with hepatosplenomegaly:

A May be normal

B May have congenital cytomegalovirus infection

C Should have a chromosome analysis

D Requires Hb electrophoresis

E May have a Rhesus negative mother

129 Neonatal jaundice:

A Is pathological at two hours

B Is common in breast fed babies

C Requires thyroid function tests

D May be due to sickle cell disease

E May be due to meningitis

130 β-Mimetics used for tocolysis are associated with:

[A] Hyperglycaemia

[B] Hypertension

[C] Pyrexia

[D] Pulmonary oedema

[E] Renal failure

Answers

1   [A]- **True**   [B]- False   [C]- **True**   [D]- **True**   [E]- False

Blood pressure falls in the first trimester despite the increase in cardiac output. This is because of a marked drop in peripheral resistance. This fall in peripheral resistance is refractory to angiotensin II and the abolition of this response has been used in the past to predict subsequent hypertension. Arm circumference above 35 cm is not common. A blood pressure in the right arm with the patient lying on the left side will seem to be lower than the reading taken when she lies flat on her back. If the patient stands peripheral resistance will increase and so will diastolic pressure. The cuff must be positioned at the level of the heart and blood pressure is best taken in the semi-prone position. In the third trimester one reading of 140/90 occurs in 20% of women and therefore on one occasion is not a good discriminator of normality.

2   [A]- **True**   [B]- **True**   [C]- False   [D]- False   [E]- **True**

Structural abnormalities of the brain are easily identified on ultrasound at 20 weeks. Gastroschisis is distinguished from exomphalos and both are causes of a raised serum alphafetoprotein. Infantile polycystic kidneys can be identified on ultrasound at 20 weeks, but many cases do not present till later in pregnancy or even rarely in the newborn. Therefore it is not possible to exclude the diagnosis at 20 weeks. Cardiac abnormalities are picked up on the four chamber view at 20 weeks.

3 $\boxed{A}$– False $\boxed{B}$– **True** $\boxed{C}$– **True** $\boxed{D}$– **True** $\boxed{E}$– False

Aminophylline and steroids are standard treatments for severe attacks of asthma and must not be withheld in the pregnant woman. Bronchospasm can be a feature of pulmonary embolus which is more common in pregnancy than in the non-pregnant. Prostaglandin E_2 has theoretical vasoconstrictor effect on the bronchus, but in practice this is not usually a problem with careful induction of labour.

4 $\boxed{A}$– False $\boxed{B}$– False $\boxed{C}$– False $\boxed{D}$– **True** $\boxed{E}$– **True**

Hypertensive disease remains the commonest cause of maternal death. Thromboembolic disease is generally quoted to have a 10% recurrent risk. It is important to make a diagnosis and venography and lung scanning can be used. The fetus can be shielded. Subcutaneous heparin can be used to treat thromboembolism and thrombocytopenia is a recognised complication.

5 $\boxed{A}$– **True** $\boxed{B}$– False $\boxed{C}$– **True** $\boxed{D}$– **True** $\boxed{E}$– False

In practice 10 g may be a better cut-off for abnormality, and iron deficiency is diagnosed by a high total iron binding capacity and low serum ferritin. There is no evidence that iron is of benefit to all pregnant women as the only proven benefit is to increase iron stores. It is therefore more appropriate to search for anaemia rather than to treat all women with iron as they may develop side-effects.

6   [A]– False   [B]– True   [C]– True   [D]– True   [E]– True

Only if the Apgar score is still 3 at 20 minutes will there be a 50% chance of subsequent cerebral palsy. However 75% of children with cerebral palsy have a 5 minute Apgar score of 7 or greater. Continuous electronic monitoring does reduce the risk of seizures, but whether this translates into a reduction in neurological deficit is uncertain.

7   [A]– True   [B]– False   [C]– True   [D]– True   [E]– True

Phenylketonuria is inherited as an autosomal recessive.

8   [A]– False   [B]– True   [C]– True   [D]– True   [E]– False

Half of the cases of shoulder dystocia occur in infants weighing less than 4 kg. Furthermore ultrasound assessment of weight at the large end of fetal weight is relatively inaccurate. Therefore this should not be used as a reference to determine mode of delivery. Primary dysfunctional labour is not due to dystocia in most cases.

9   [A]– True   [B]– True   [C]– True   [D]– True   [E]– True

Meconium stained liquor in labour is associated with a five-fold increase in perinatal death. Much of this can be reduced by Caesarean section, but identifying the baby at specific risk remains difficult. There is much data to suggest that booking of low-risk primigravida for Consultant units increases the rate of Caesarean section for such women. Much of this is probably due to continuous electronic monitoring which, despite the use of fetal blood sampling, remains a cause of increased Caesarean sections. Secondary arrest of labour is associated with dystocia, although data from Kings College Hospital dispute this.

10   A - False   B - True   C - True   D - True   E - True

Ergometrine should not be used for prophylaxis in the active management of the third stage of labour, as it is no more effective than oxytocin and is associated with a greater risk of hypertension vomiting. 90% of post-partum haemorrhage is due to uterine atony.

11   A - False   B - False   C - True   D - True   E - True

IUDs protect against pregnancy, and therefore the overall risk is lower than in women not using any contraception. However a woman who becomes pregnant with an IUD in situ has a higher risk of an ectopic pregnancy. Concomitant ectopic and intrauterine pregnancies have been described, particularly after assisted conception programmes. Many now regard laparoscopic salpingostomy as the standard treatment of choice, although this does lead to a small recurrence risk. However the subsequent pregnancy rate would appear to be higher than after salpingectomy. Serum HCG measurements are highly sensitive.

12   A - True   B - False   C - False   D - True   E - False

Smoking rather than age is the risk factor identified with contraceptive pill usage, and particularly with the new progestagens continued use is safe up to and even over the age of 40. There is some protection from ovarian cancer, endometrial cancer and dysfunctional bleeding, and these are some of the health benefits of oral contraception.

13 [A]- False [B]- **True** [C]- False [D]- **True** [E]- **True**

Size and growth are not the same, and many babies of appropriate weight for gestation may be growth retarded. Such a diagnosis requires assessment of ponderal index. About 10% of such babies have minimal cerebral dysfunction with learning and speech difficulties.

14 [A]- **True** [B]- **True** [C]- **True** [D]- **Truc** [E]- False

Mild to moderate hyperstimulation is very common in assisted cycles and is particularly common if pregnancy ensues. Nevertheless it may be avoided by not giving the HCG if it is suspected. Pleural effusion is common but laparotomy is only required for haemorrhage of the ovarian cyst, which is very rare.

15 [A]- False [B]- **True** [C]- False [D]- **True** [E]- False

Only 25% of women with polycystic ovary syndrome are obese, and fertility is not altered by the use of the contraceptive pill before pregnancy. Treatment with the contraceptive pill reduces the stimulation of the ovaries by LH and lessens the symptoms of acne, hirsutism and weight gain. LH secretion is pulsatile and multiple blood tests may need to be performed.

16 [A]- False [B]- **True** [C]- False [D]- False [D]- False

Tumour volume and stage are the most significant prognostic factors. Young age is often said to be an adverse factor, but stage for stage prognosis seems to be similar.

17 [A]- True [B]- True [C]- True [D]- False [E]- False

Response rate with platinum is no more than 20%.
Exenterative surgery still has a place but only if the tumour is central with no evidence of pelvic side of distant metastasis. The prognosis for advanced/recurrent carcinoma of the cervix is poor.

18 [A]- False [B]- True [C]- True [D]- False [E]- False

Despite one study from Scandinavia suggesting reduced fertility most evidence does not confirm this. In cases of suspicion of malignancy in pregnancy wedge biopsy of the abnormal area is preferable as haemorrhage can be difficult to control. Adequate cone biopsy can be performed under local anaesthetic with either laser or loop diathermy. Glandular abnormalities need sampling of the endometrium as well as the endocervix.

19 [A]- True [B]- False [C]- False [D]- False [E]- False

Less than 5% of such women will have positive para-aortic nodes and there is no agreed management of these patients. Conservation of the ovaries is still appropriate in adenocarcinoma and neoadjuvant chemotherapy is indicated only in randomised trials. Radiotherapy may be indicated with positive lymph nodes although this does not improve survival but only disease-free interval.

20 [A]– False [B]– False [C]– True [D]– False [E]– True

Approximately 20% of patients with advanced disease will ultimately die from it. Borderline tumours, whilst generally benign, do have a mortality rate. Chemotherapy has not been shown to have been of use even in implant disease. Such implants are best excised. Aneuploidy is associated with poorer prognosis.

21 [A]– False [B]– True [C]– False [D]– True [E]– False

Whilst surgery has a major part to play in early disease its place in advanced disease remains controversial. Platinum therapy however is clearly shown to have a survival advantage. The only studies to investigate hormone replacement therapy have shown no deleterious effect, but whether this is a real effect remains unclear. The rate of fall of Ca125 is of prognostic value but second laparotomy no longer has a place.

22 [A]– False [B]– False [C]– False [D]– True [E]– True

The most important prognostic factors are the intervals since the antecedent pregnancy, the adequate response to chemotherapy and the site and number of metastases. The commonest cause of death is drug resistance and etoposide is one of the most active agents, possibly even more active than methotrexate.

23 [A]– True [B]– True [C]– True [D]– False [E]– False

The staging has changed from clinical assessment to surgical and requires assessment of the myometrial depth. HRT is commonly said to be contraindicated but there is not a great deal of published data to support this. If anything the data available suggests that outcome is improved, presumably because patients are cured and HRT prevents osteoporosis and arterial disease. Post-operative irradiation of the vault is better than pre-operative.

24   [A]– False   [B]– **True**   [C]– False   [D]– False   [E]– False

Pelvic lymphadenectomy is no longer required in vulval cancer as there is good evidence that pelvic radiotherapy is more effective. Lesions of 5 mm have a significant risk of lymph node metastases and inguino-femoral lymphadenectomy is still required. It has been suggested that at least three inguinal nodes should be positive before considering adjuvant radiotherapy, although not all accept this. The depth of invasion is not easily measured due to variation in keratin thickness and has to be measured from the top of the most superficial dermal papilla and/or the point of origin of the invasive cells if this can be established with confidence.

25   [A]– False   [B]– **True**   [C]– **True**   [D]– False   [E]– **True**

Arterial pCO_2 levels fall but the mechanism is uncertain. Whether this is due to the increase in respiratory tidal volume and capacity, or whether these changes are consequent on a lower CO_2, is unknown.

26   [A]– False   [B]– False   [C]– **True**   [D]– **True**   [E]– **True**

3rd degree tears involve the anal sphincter and 4th degree tears the anal mucosa. Controlled studies show the frequency of 3rd degree tears to be equally common in the episiotomy and intention to avoid episiotomy groups. Such tears must be repaired under a good light with proper analgesia under either regional or general anaesthesia. Recent ultrasound assessments have shown a large degree of sphincter incompetence at three months although this does not always imply a lack of continence. Ventouse is the instrument of first choice because of the reduction in maternal morbidity, and a recto-vaginal fistula cannot always be avoided even with expert repair. This is one of the reasons for preventing this damage in the first place.

27 [A]– False   [B]– **True**   [C]– **True**   [D]– False   [E]– **True**

Vomiting is commonly due to pyelonephritis in the first trimester but the normal hormonal changes probably account for the majority of cases. Appendicitis must always be considered but in intractable cases of hyperemesis steroids have been shown to be of use.

28 [A]– False   [B]– False   [C]– **True**   [D]– **True**   [E]– **True**

Antibiotics may be of use but this is still being assessed by the ORACLE study (Overview of the Role of Antibiotics in Curtailing Labour and Early Delivery) to which such patients should be entered. Steroids should be given, as the greatest risk is of prematurity. Treatment of group B streptococcus is of value in preventing neonatal morbidity only if it is continued through labour. A baby that is showing signs of being infected should be delivered as soon as possible as the extra 12 hours of labour seriously jeopardise its chances of survival.

29 [A]– False   [B]– False   [C]– False   [D]– **True**   [E]– **True**

Omphalocoele has a strong association with Trisomy 18 (50%) and cystic hygroma is strongly associated with Turner's syndrome (70%). Choroid plexus cysts and a dilated renal pelvis are an indication for anomaly scanning but in themselves do not carry a risk high enough alone to justify fetal sampling in general practice.

30 [A]- **True** [B]- **True** [C]- False [D]- False [E]- False

Rheumatoid arthritis often improves in pregnancy due to the rise in steroid levels. Migraine is often cyclical and will tend to improve. Multiple sclerosis and epilepsy show no consistent relationship with pregnancy.

31 [A]- **True** [B]- **True** [C]- **True** [D]- **True** [E]- **True**

The trophoblast infiltration during placentation is thought to be essential to dilate the arterioles and expand the uteroplacental blood flow. Atherosis is the aggregation of fibrinogen, platelets and lipophages which partially or completely block the arteries. Both effects can occur with intrauterine growth retardation without pre-eclampsia. Arteries have an increased sensitivity to angiotensin II which is abolished in a normal pregnancy. Endothelial cell swelling leads to endotheliosis and circulating blood volume is reduced.

32 [A]- False [B]- **True** [C]- False [D]- False [E]- False

For unexplained reasons pre-eclampsia appears to be less in smokers, but genetic analysis does suggest a single recessive trait. There is no difference in incidence with the type of twinning and anti-hypertensive therapy is used for blood pressure control, not to alter the course of the disease. Phenytoin is not a good anticonvulsant, and when required diazepam is the commonest drug in the UK. Magnesium sulphate is becoming more popular in the UK as its efficacy is well known in other parts of the world where eclampsia is more common.

33 [A]– True   [B]– True   [C]– True   [D]– True   [E]– True

Blindness can be due to many mechanisms including central arterial and venous thrombosis and retinal oedema and detachment. Fundoscopy is part of the assessment of such patients. Microangiopathic haemolysis occurs in the general coagulopathy of pre-eclampsia including thrombocytopenia. Liver failure is a late manifestation.

34 [A]– False   [B]– True   [C]– True   [D]– False   [E]– True

The dose of aspirin given was 60 mg and it did show a statistical increase in post-partum haemorrhage and post delivery blood transfusion. Nevertheless this was small and in clinical practice may not be relevant. The only definite benefit from low dose aspirin is in women whose previous problems have started before 32 weeks and overall the study does not encourage the use of aspirin outside this small group of women.

35 [A]– True   [B]– False   [C]– False   [D]– False   [E]– True

Recent randomised control trials have confirmed the efficacy of ECV in reducing the risk of Caesarean section. The risk to the fetus appears minimal but larger studies are still awaited. This treatment should be offered to women with a breech presentation but it should take place in the antenatal ward under tocolytic control and with all the facilities available for assessment of the fetus once the treatment has been performed. In the early stages of labour it can still be performed. There remains no good evidence to offer Caesarean section to all breech presentations, although this is becoming an increasing trend. The exclusion of a fetal abnormality is mandatory.

36 [A]– True   [B]– False   [C]– False   [D]– True   [E]– False

Women losing 80 ml of blood per month must become anaemic and therefore haemoglobin is a reasonably reliable indicator of blood loss. Similarly the number of towels and tampons used varies from woman to woman and is not a good indicator of blood loss. Cyklokapron has a specific effect by inhibiting plasminogen activation and fibrinolysis. It is very effective in genuine menorrhagia and can be prescribed indefinitely as the restriction on use has recently been lifted.

37 [A]– False   [B]– True   [C]– True   [D]– False   [E]– False

The use of antibiotics prophylactically with indwelling catheters leads to resistant strains of organisms and is to be avoided. If infection occurs removal of the catheter is prudent if possible, but the prescription of antibiotics is required only in the presence of a temperature or pyuria. Intermittent clean self-catheterisation results in less infection.

38 [A]– True   [B]– True   [C]– True   [D]– True   [E]– False

Dexamethasone is the treatment for hirsutism due to adrenal causes and the oral contraceptive pill for ovarian causes. The human hair growth cycle is at least six months long and therefore therapy requires a minimum of six months before useful assessment can be made. Raised DHEA suggests an adrenal cause of hirsutism.

39 [A]– False   [B]– True   [C]– True   [D]– False   [E]– True

The American fertility score is particularly useful in comparative studies and to assess the result of treatment. 200 mg of danazol may well be as effective as larger doses and there is evidence that amenorrhoea is not required. Results of medical treatment are good, particularly with the use of GnRH analogues. Endometriosis is due to retrograde menstruation and therefore cannot occur *de novo* after sterilisation.

40 [A]- False [B]- False [C]- True [D]- True [E]- True

The vast majority of cases are dysfunctional and clotting disorders are extremely uncommon. Problems at this early age often herald menstrual problems later in life, but the contraceptive pill remains a very good long-term treatment.

41 [A]- True [B]- False [C]- False [D]- True [E]- True

The risk of infection is very low in the United Kingdom population. The risk of infection is increased by induction due to the increased number of vaginal examinations. Furthermore Caesarean section is commoner and, if anything, the risk to the fetus is greater than awaiting spontaneous labour which occurs in 90% of women within 48 hours.

42 [A]- False [B]- False [C]- False [D]- False [E]- True

X-ray pelvimetry is of no value in predicting who will deliver normally, and if there have been two previous Caesarean sections for non-recurrent indications then attempts at further vaginal delivery have been shown to be as safe as after one Caesarean. Asymptomatic women after delivery should not have potentially dangerous manipulations of the uterus. Whilst often quoted as a reason to deny future trials of labour the occurrence of a post-operative infection has not been shown in controlled studies to be related to future problems.

43 $\boxed{A}$ – **True** $\boxed{B}$ – False $\boxed{C}$ – False $\boxed{D}$ – **True** $\boxed{E}$ – False

Colposuspension supports the bladder neck and the base of the bladder, whereas a Stamey procedure only supports the bladder neck. Sacrocolpopexy will support the vault only and anterior repair will also be required for cystocoele. The same applies with a sling operation.

44 $\boxed{A}$ – **True** $\boxed{B}$ – **True** $\boxed{C}$ – False $\boxed{D}$ – False $\boxed{E}$ – False

Radical hysterectomy is commonly associated with an atonic bladder and the need for it to be regularly emptied by catheterisation. Colposuspension is associated with an obstructive element and the possible need for self-catheterisation. Catheterisation should be discussed with all women before surgery. The other operations are not associated with an obstructive element and long-term bladder problems are not described.

45 $\boxed{A}$ – **True** $\boxed{B}$ – **True** $\boxed{C}$ – **True** $\boxed{D}$ – **True** $\boxed{E}$ – False

It is not clear why 25% of women suffer no vasomotor symptoms but norethisterone has been shown to be of benefit and can be useful in the small number of women in whom oestrogen is contraindicated. HRT does not predispose to thrombosis and therefore may still be given to women with a previous history after careful discussion.

46 $\boxed{A}$ – False $\boxed{B}$ – **True** $\boxed{C}$ – **True** $\boxed{D}$ – **True** $\boxed{E}$ – **True**

HRT means that women should be treated as if they were pre-menopausal and there is no need to stop HRT prior to surgery. Norethisterone in theory may counteract some of the benefits of oestrogen replacement therapy, but this has not been proven in practice. Serum levels are considerably lower than in the premenopausal range and therefore can be given at low dose to prevent symptoms. Some women may respond to continuous progestagen as the stopping and starting of norethisterone may be associated with switching on and off of progesterone receptors and exacerbating symptoms.

47 [A]– True   [B]– False   [C]– False   [D]– True   [E]– True

IUDs should be removed in pregnancy to reduce the risk of septic abortion. Ultrasound is the best method of locating 'lost' coils. Actinomyces should initially be treated with penicillin and the coil changed if it is due. However, the coil does not need to be removed permanently. The duration of use does not increase the risk of infertility.

48 [A]– False   [B]– True   [C]– False   [D]– True   [E]– False

The use for IUI is controversial and many would say is only indicated in erectile and ejaculatory disorders. 90% of conceptions occur within two years. The treatment of varicocoeles has not been shown in controlled trials to improve fertility, and age is the most important factor when fertility is unexplained. Congenital occlusion of the vas is often associated with defective sperm function.

49 [A]– True   [B]– True   [C]– False   [D]– True   [E]– True

The risk of miscarriage after confirmation of a pregnancy on ultrasound is of the order of 5% and would account for the value of reassurance after the pregnancy has been confirmed and the difficulty in proving the effectiveness of any of the other proposed therapies. Any infectious disease can result in spontaneous miscarriage.

50 [A]– False [B]– True [C]– False [D]– False [E]– True

The average age of the menopause in the UK is 52 years and smoking is one of the influences on this age, but others include racial origin, family history and parity. Total cholesterol levels rise due to a rise in low-density lipoprotein. Plasma triglycerides rise, but this is also an age-dependent factor. Ovarian biopsy is not required for a diagnosis of premature menopause and there is some evidence that hysterectomy in some women may initiate the menopause, presumably due to interference with ovarian blood supply.

51 [A]– False [B]– True [C]– False [D]– True [E]– True

Serial vaginal examinations are not indicated and even if changes in the cervix are recognised there is no evidence of effective intervention. There are sufficient data from randomised studies to show that routine use of anti-D at 28 weeks of pregnancy for all Rhesus-negative women is of value in reducing the risk of sensitisation, particularly in primigravidae. However the cost of such a programme is high and supplies of anti-D have been limited. There is no evidence that the involvement of a Consultant in the care of all women is required, but it should be available for specific indications and if the mothers request. Mothers are less likely to lose their notes than is the hospital. Although the risk of transmission of hepatitis B from HBsAg-positive mothers is less in Europeans than in Chinese, post-natal vaccination of neonates in all HBeAg-positive mothers is recommended. It would therefore seem much easier to screen all women for hepatitis B than to target specific groups, which may appear racist.

52 [A]– False [B]– False [C]– True [D]– False [E]– True

Whilst a reduction in fetal movements is predictive of antepartum late death it is still unclear whether this predicts such a death at a time when it would be possible to avert the outcome. The large randomised studies available suggest that intervention may have been delayed and that this is the cause of the lack of efficacy rather than the test itself. The suggestion is that less than 1:1000 might benefit from fetal movement counting and that the implication for using this test on all women must be taken into account. Doppler ultrasound is able to predict fetal distress in labour, but this is only applicable to high risk pregnancies such as pre-eclampsia. The prevention of pre-term birth is the biggest hope for improving perinatal mortality from an obstetric point of view, but there is no evidence that this is likely in the near future. The Caesarean section rate will not improve perinatal mortality, but induction of labour at 41+ weeks has shown a small benefit.

53 [A]– True [B]– False [C]– True [D]– True [E]– True

The risk of transfer of the virus from mother to fetus was probably overestimated initially and a large European study has shown that 75% of babies born to HIV positive mothers will have lost their maternal antibody by 12 months. Therefore providing the mother is well and does not have viraemia the risk is less than previously thought. There is an increased incidence of CIN and breastfeeding is not advisable.

54   [A]– False   [B]– True   [C]– True   [D]– True   [E]– False

The Pill protects against ovarian cancer and endometriosis and should be recommended to women with a family history of ovarian cancer. It also gives protection against pelvic inflammatory disease but its relationship with breast cancer and cervical intraepithelial neoplasia is more controversial. There is some epidemiological evidence that it will increase the risk of breast cancer.

55   [A]– False   [B]– True   [C]– True   [D]– True   [E]– False

Twice as many males as females are affected by talipes and 90% of affected infants with CDH are female. Isolated cleft palate is commoner in females but cleft palate associated with cleft lip is commoner in males. 80% of infants with pyloric stenosis are male and the same applies to Hirschsprung's disease.

56   [A]– True   [B]– True   [C]– True   [D]– True   [E]– True

Manic depressive illness may be exacerbated and confused with premenstrual syndrome. Prospective symptom charts are essential for diagnosis and fail to confirm it in 50% of cases. Premenstrual syndrome is improved by hysterectomy alone although the mechanism is unclear. Enthusiasm therefore for bilateral salpingo-oophorectomy in all women with premenstrual syndrome should be contained and reserved for severe cases.

57 [A]– True [B]– True [C]– True [D]– False [E]– False

High dose progestagens do suppress pituitary gonadotrophins and therefore ovulation ceases. The effects may last up to two years on stopping, depending on how long the drug has been used. HDL levels are reduced and this appears to be due to the androgenic properties rather than the progestagenic ones. The clinical importance of this is uncertain. Progestagen-only contraception is ideal for diabetics and hypertensives.

58 [A]– False [B]– True [C]– False [D]– True [E]– True

The miscarriage rate with chorionic villus biopsy is quoted as 2–4% and therefore triple screening is preferable for maternal age alone. Nevertheless the risk can be discussed if there are other reasons for considering an early diagnosis. There has been concern for limb deformities if the test is performed before 10 weeks.

59 [A]– False [B]– False [C]– True [D]– True [E]– True

The odds of an affected fetus are related to the local prevalence rate but there is no point in repeating the test as a different result will cause confusion and possibly delay in proceeding to definitive diagnosis. There is an increased risk of a low-birth-weight baby but the test is not sufficiently accurate for clinical use. Women with insulin-dependent diabetes tend to have a low maternal serum AFP and thus a high risk of a pregnancy affected by a neural tube defect. Therefore a cut-off lower than that in the general population is used for screening.

60 [A]- **True** [B]- False [C]- False [D]- False [E]- **True**

Azithromycin is a useful antibiotic with wide coverage including chlamydia. Acute inflammatory disease can still occur in pregnancy and therefore a positive pregnancy test does not exclude it. Evidence is accumulating that one infection with chlamydia, perhaps because of the difficulty and delay in diagnosis, can lead to subsequent infertility in at least 20% of women. Diagnosis often requires laparoscopy and tubal culture for confirmation, and this is one of the reasons it is very difficult to accurately assess the true prevalence and sequelae of acute inflammatory disease.

61 [A]- False [B]- False [C]- False [D]- False [E]- False

The amount of warfarin excreted in the breast milk is minimal. Breast feeding should not be relied on for contraception as ovulation can occur before the first period. There is no requirement to encourage extra fluids when breastfeeding, and feeding should be continued with mastitis as this will tend to reduce the risk of progress to infection and abscess formation. There is no evidence that antenatal nipple care is important and if the problem is identified this may detract some women from attempting to breast feed later.

62 [A]- False [B]- **True** [C]- False [D]- False [E]- **True**

Routine glucose tolerance testing is not an effective form of care in pregnancy and childbirth, and the fasting blood sugar will be useful according to WHO guidelines. One of the problems with gestational diabetes is that the oral glucose tolerance test is poorly reproducible and will give different results when repeated after only one or two days. However there is a definite syndrome of gestational diabetes but the true prevalence and standards for diagnosis remain to be defined.

63 [A]- **True**   [B]- **True**   [C]- **True**   [D]- **True**   [E]- False

Successful drug treatment of detrusor instability often produces severe side-effects, particularly dry mouth, and this tolerance to side-effects is the dose-limiting factor. The association of prolapse with incontinence is difficult but urgency may be improved by anterior repair, particularly if the prolapse is marked. Cystoscopy is indicated and those with normal findings are often improved by bladder distension and urethral dilatation. Clam cystoplasty may be an operation worth considering in sensory urgency.

64 [A]- **True**   [B]- False   [C]- **True**   [D]- False   [E]- **True**

Urethral pressure profiles are not useful in diagnosis and only cystometry is required before surgery to exclude detrusor instability. Urodynamics can effectively be performed by a nurse although more complicated investigations will undoubtedly require a medical input.

65 [A]- **True**   [B]- **True**   [C]- **True**   [D]- **True**   [E]- **True**

It is important to measure flow rates before colposuspension as a poor flow indicates a relatively atonic detrusor muscle which will lead to problems with retention in the long term post-operatively. Inversion of the vagina may cause obstruction and may require replacement before adequate emptying of the bladder is achieved.

66 [A]– False [B]– **True** [C]– False [D]– False [E]– **True**

The mean duration of lochia is ´33 days with 33% of women still having persistent loss at 60 days. Curettage is a dangerous procedure and most cases of retained products will present within two weeks. Approximately 1:30 000 pregnancies in the UK are followed by choriocarcinoma. In the non-breastfeeding woman, commencement on the contraceptive pill will help post-partum bleeding.

67 [A]– **True** [B]– False [C]– **True** [D]– False [E]– **True**

As many as 10% of non pregnant and 40% of pregnant women may have vaginal colonisation with *Candida*. *Candida* typically occurs after menses due to the change in vaginal pH. The woman's partner should be tested as carriage is not uncommon, particularly in the non-circumcised.

68 [A]– False [B]– **True** [C]– **True** [D]– False [E]– False

Drug resistance is not a problem but non-*albicans* strains can occur. Daily ketoconazole is better treatment in recurrent infection but negative microscopy may be followed by a positive culture.

69 [A]– **True** [B]– False [C]– False [D]– False [E]– **True**

The presence of lesions in early labour may be an indication for Caesarean section, because of the risk of local contamination. Routine cultures are not reliable and results often take several days to come through. Even if a positive culture is obtained at 37 weeks the virus may have stopped shedding by 41 weeks when the woman goes into labour. At least half of neonatal infections give no maternal history.

70 [A]- **True**   [B]- False   [C]- **True**   [D]- False   [E]- False

Podophylline is contraindicated in pregnancy, and not treating warts merely leads to rapid growth in the third trimester.

71 [A]- False   [B]- False   [C]- False   [D]- **True**   [E]- **True**

The risk of infection with toxoplasmosis is highest in the third trimester, when the risk of serious fetal effects is lowest. Only 14% of transmissions in the first trimester lead to fetal effects and recommendations for termination may be unnecessary. Spiromycin is not an effective treatment, although it is widely used in France. Attention should be paid to hygiene rather than to a screening programme.

72 [A]- False   [B]- **True**   [C]- **True**   [D]- **True**   [E]- **True**

Vulval herpes often presents with retention of urine, when it is best treated by suprapubic catheterisation. Retention due to retroverted uterus in pregnancy is best treated by urethral catheterisation and waiting for the uterus to move out of the pelvis.

73 [A]- **True**   [B]- False   [C]- False   [D]- **True**   [E]- **True**

Up to 8% of pregnant women harbour bacteriuria at booking and as many as 40% of these will progress to symptomatic urinary tract infection if untreated. Oral antibiotics are effective unless the woman is vomiting and there is little evidence to support continued use throughout the pregnancy. Two doses of 3 g ampicillin are required but compliance is usually better than with a seven-day course.

74 |A|- **True** |B|- **True** |C|- False |D|- **True** |E|- False

Herpes virus can be seen only by electron microscopy, and although evidence of HPV infection may be manifest by koilocytes the organism itself is not detectable on a smear.

75 |A|- False |B|- False |C|- **True** |D|- **True** |E|- False

The gene frequency of cystic fibrosis is 1:20 and it is the commonest genetic disorder in Caucasians. This results in a birth incidence of 1:2000 live births.

76 |A|- False |B|- **True** |C|- **True** |D|- False |E|- **True**

The evidence for antenatal surveillance by physical testing is poor and induction of labour has been shown to reduce the risk of late perinatal death. Post-maturity is a syndrome of babies identifiable only after birth.

77 |A|- False |B|- **True** |C|- **True** |D|- **True** |E|- False

Routine intubation is not recommended but rather attendance by a trained paediatrician who can decide whether this is indicated or not. The routine use of sodium bicarbonate has not been shown to be of value.

78 |A|- **True** |B|- False |C|- **True** |D|- False |E|- False

The main benefit of routine ultrasound is the reduction in the incidence of post dates pregnancies. It is an essential part of triple screening as most tests rely on biparietal diameter for calculating the gestation. Whilst ultrasound has not been shown to be associated with any definite dangers the alternative is still the case, i.e. it has not been shown to be unsafe.

79 $\boxed{\text{A}}$– False $\boxed{\text{B}}$– False $\boxed{\text{C}}$– False $\boxed{\text{D}}$– **True** $\boxed{\text{E}}$– False

GnRH analogues initially stimulate the pituitary and cannot be used for more than six months due to the effect of low oestrogen on bone. They result in a low FSH/LH and can be used in young women with endometriosis or in IVF cycles.

80 $\boxed{\text{A}}$– False $\boxed{\text{B}}$– False $\boxed{\text{C}}$– False $\boxed{\text{D}}$– False $\boxed{\text{E}}$– False

Transverse lie may be recurrent due to an abnormality in the uterus but most cases revert to cephalic after 37 weeks. If this is the case then spontaneous labour should be awaited. At delivery it is best to perform external version before incising the uterus as this can avoid the necessity for complex incisions on the uterus. If problems arise then the transverse incision should be extended laterally and upwards as a J rather than as an inverted T which may result in necrosis in a future pregnancy.

81 $\boxed{\text{A}}$– **True** $\boxed{\text{B}}$– False $\boxed{\text{C}}$– False $\boxed{\text{D}}$– False $\boxed{\text{E}}$– False

Tetracycline causes dental discoloration only when there are teeth, i.e. the third trimester. Metronidazole does not have specific fetal effects and aminoglycosides cause 8th cranial nerve damage. Warfarin is safe during lactation but phenindione should be avoided. The predominant toxic effect of azathioprine is myelosuppression.

82 [A]– **True** [B]– **True** [C]– False [D]– **True** [E]– False

Amiodarone should be avoided as it is present in the milk in significant amounts and it releases iodine which raises the possibility of neonatal goitre. Bloody diarrhoea and rashes have been reported with maternal ingestion of sulphasalazine and carbimazole may be sufficient to also affect the neonatal thyroid.

83 [A]– **True** [B]– **True** [C]– **True** [D]– **True** [E]– False

Enterocoele can be difficult to demonstrate and dynamic proctography is the most useful test available. At abdominal surgery Halban's technique is better than the Moskovitz procedure as there is less risk to the ureter. Enterocoele can occur anterior to the vaginal vault after hysterectomy, although this is rare.

84 [A]– False [B]– **True** [C]– False [D]– **True** [E]– False

Distinguishing squamous metaplasia from CIN requires experience but the intensity of acetic acid staining is suspicious of CIN 3 at least. Destructive therapy has not been completely replaced as large loop excision is not indicated in all cases of abnormal smear. CIN 1 may often revert back to normal and radical hysterectomy should be performed as soon as possible after a diagnosis of invasive carcinoma.

85 [A]– False [B]– **True** [C]– **True** [D]– **True** [E]– **True**

Approximately 2% of colonised babies develop serious disease and the use of prophylactic penicillin increases the rate of sepsis due to penicillin resistant organisms. Increased death rates have been reported. Antibiotics are effective in the mother only if given during labour, and the best hope of eradicating haemolytic streptococci is to be able to offer a routine test in labour for all women.

86 [A]– **True** [B]– **True** [C]– **True** [D]– **True** [E]– **True**

The sickle cell syndromes include sickle cell trait HBAS, homozygous HBSS and compound heterozygotes for Hb variants, the most important of which is HBSC disease. Spontaneous miscarriage and premature delivery rate are at least twice that of the normal population, and small-for-dates is also common. Regional anaesthesia may predispose to sickling by pooling in the extremities.

87 [A]– **True** [B]– **True** [C]– False [D]– False [E]– **True**

The physical signs of anorexia nervosa include hypotension bradycardia and lanugo. Serum gonadotrophins are low and fertility remains depressed. Reproductive outcome is reduced in women of low body mass index.

88 [A]– True   [B]– True   [C]– True   [D]– True   [E]– True

Most cases will respond to supportive therapy but severe post-natal depression requiring admission to a psychiatric mother and baby unit affects 1 in 1000 women. The recurrence rate may be as high as 1:10 but this is reduced if the next pregnancy is delayed for at least two years. Where hospital admission is required it is usually for several months, and there is significant risk of suicide and infanticide.

89 [A]– True   [B]– True   [C]– True   [D]– False   [E]– False

Osteoporosis and stress fractures are common in amenorrhoeic athletes. Menstruation depends on the amount of body fat. However serum FSH should be measured to be sure that there are not other causes for amenorrhoea. Fertility should return to normal with an increase in body mass index. There is no reason for athletes to avoid the contraceptive pill.

90 [A]– True   [B]– False   [C]– False   [D]– False   [E]– False

Lichen sclerosis has recently been shown to have a high association with later malignancy but whether follow up of all women with this condition is practical remains uncertain. High dose steroids (i.e. Dermovate) are the best treatment available as vulvectomy inevitably leads to recurrence.

91 [A]– True   [B]– True   [C]– True   [D]– True   [E]– False

Clomiphene causes hot flushes due to its anti-oestrogen effect on the hypothalamus. The manufacturers recommend searching for other causes if pregnancy has not been achieved within six months, although an adverse effect on the cervical mucus is one of the reasons. There is an increased incidence of twin pregnancies but not any more than this.

92 [A]– False [B]– **True** [C]– False [D]– False [E]– False

Urinary excretion of iodide doubles due to a reduction in renal tubular absorption. This leads to a fall in the plasma level and the thyroid gland is forced to triple its iodine uptake from the blood. Thyroid disease is familial and thyroid stimulating immunoglobulin may still be raised in euthyroid women on treatment. Such antibodies cross the placenta and can lead to neonatal thyrotoxicosis. It is rare for surgery to be required in pregnancy and medical treatment is preferable.

93 [A]– **True** [B]– False [C]– False [D]– **True** [E]– **True**

A fall in creatinine clearance in the third trimester is not necessarily abnormal but should be monitored carefully. Immunosuppressive treatment does not need to be routinely increased but adjustments may be necessary if there is a decrease in maternal white blood count. Long-term use of antibiotics has not been shown to have been beneficial. Most preterm deliveries are due to obstetric intervention associated with poor renal function.

94 [A]– False [B]– **True** [C]– **True** [D]– **True** [E]– False

Osteoporosis traditionally is defined clinically by the occurrence of a typical fracture which would not have been sufficient to break normal bone. Pathologically there is reduced bone mass per unit volume of bone, but otherwise the bone is normal. There is evidence that oestrogen can result in some gaining of bone density.

95 **A**– True **B**– True **C**– True **D**– False **E**– True

Pelvic ultrasound is useful and as well as showing upper pelvic anatomy should show the presence of cryptomenorrhoea. Chromosomes will indicate the possibility of testicular feminisation syndrome but serum oestradiol is not of use.

96 **A**– True **B**– True **C**– False **D**– False **E**– True

Great care must be taken when prescribing in women with acute porphyria. Progestagens are probably more hazardous than oestrogens. The progesterone-only pill does not inhibit ovulation although long-term Depoprovera usually does.

97 **A**– True **B**– True **C**– False **D**– True **E**– True

FSH and LH levels may be useful especially in the absence of normal sexual characteristics or negative progesterone challenge test. Albright's syndrome is associated with polyostotic fibrodysplasia and fractures of long bones. Breast buds are the first sign of puberty and GnRH analogues can be useful in treatment although they are not always required.

98 **A**– True **B**– False **C**– True **D**– True **E**– True

Mebendazole is appropriate treatment for threadworms, a common cause of pruritus in children. Most cases, however, are due to under-oestrogenisation of the vagina and respond to attention to hygiene. Oestrogen cream is occasionally of use, but antibiotics are not indicated.

99 | A - True | B - True | C - True | D - False | E - True

Hypercalcaemia is found in 8–10% of terminally ill patients whether or not they have bone metastases. TENS is sometimes effective for localised pain and the use of a pain clinic is helpful. Cordotomy is indicated only in patients with limited life expectancy since it is never permanent. Opiate usage seldom produces confusion, and impaired renal function due to ureteric obstruction is more likely.

100 | A - False | B - False | C - False | D - True | E - True

Surgery can usually be avoided in advanced ovarian cancer as obstruction is usually at multiple levels. A colostomy is likely to be the only procedure feasible which is not generally good palliation. Patients can be kept for several months in complete obstruction of the lower gut although upper gut obstruction is not so easy to manage this way. Shunts are not indicated in weak cachectic patients.

101 | A - False | B - True | C - False | D - True | E - True

Prostaglandins are made by all cells except for red blood cells. PGE_2 relaxes the myometrium in the non-pregnant but contracts it in the pregnant. Metabolism is via the lungs. Prostacyclin I_2 is a vasodilator and inhibits platelet aggregation.

102 | A - True | B - True | C - False | D - True | E - False

Afro-Caribbeans have a reduced risk of osteoporosis but other risk factors include a late menarche, early menopause and physical inactivity.

103 [A]– False [B]– True [C]– False [D]– False [E]– False

The evidence that retinopathy deteriorates in pregnancy is controversial but women should have this possibility discussed with them. Serum fructosamine may be better than HBA1C but control should be tight rather than very tight. Induction is not routinely required at 38 weeks and the risk of the children developing diabetes is 1%, which is still much higher than the general population.

104 [A]– True [B]– False [C]– False [D]– True [E]– True

Smoking is closely associated with preterm delivery, but other factors are relevant such as social class. Fetal alcohol syndrome is associated with microcephaly and facial dysmorphism and growth retardation, as well as congenital malformations. Pyrimethamine can be used, providing adequate folate supplements are given.

105 [A]– False [B]– True [C]– False [D]– True [E]– True

0.5% of women at their first presentation for screening will have breast cancer and it has been estimated that screening in the UK will prolong the life of 1 woman in 1500, preventing 8% of all cancer at a cost of £40 000 per life.

106 [A]– False [B]– False [C]– True [D]– False [E]– False

Steroids should not be withheld in acute ulcerative colitis as this is a life threatening condition. A stool specimen is required for microbiology and culture, and a barium enema must be avoided because of the risk of perforation. Surgery may be required and should not be delayed.

107 [A]– **True** [B]– **True** [C]– False [D]– False [E]– False

SIDS is the commonest cause of death in the first year, occurring at a rate of approximately 5 per thousand. It is more likely in a sibling twin who dies from it but less common in Asian and Chinese infants. Babies should be placed supine. Smoking is relevant although other factors are important, possibly including the mattress material.

108 [A]– **True** [B]– **True** [C]– **True** [D]– **True** [E]– False

The diaphragm is effective in motivated couples, but should be used in conjunction with a spermicide. All diaphragms should be refitted at the six-week post-natal visit.

109 [A]– **True** [B]– **True** [C]– **True** [D]– **True** [E]– False

Aspirin increases the risk of bleeding due to the anti-platelet effect, but does not potentiate the warfarin *per se*. The contraceptive pill reduces the anti-coagulant effect.

110 [A]– **True** [B]– **True** [C]– **Truc** [D]– **True** [E]– False

The two occasions when normal people may hallucinate are on the edge of sleep or following bereavement. Searching behaviour is common, though not usually after perinatal death, when the child was never at home. Thought insertion is a psychotic phenomenon.

111 [A]– False [B]– **True** [C]– **True** [D]– **True** [E]– False

Post-coital contraception should be started within 72 hours but not necessarily completed. Antibiotic cover is important for women at risk of valvular heart disease.

112 [A]– True [B]– True [C]– True [D]– False [E]– False

Frusemide does cause loss of calcium but this does not lead to osteoporosis.

113 [A]– True [B]– False [C]– True [D]– False [E]– True

Perinatal mortality has fallen in diabetic pregnancy, mostly due to a reduction in unexplained/asphyxial antepartum deaths. Congenital abnormalities are varied, predominantly cardiac, skeletal and central nervous system. The incidence has not fallen despite evidence suggesting that good control is important in the first trimester.

114 [A]– False [B]– False [C]– True [D]– True [E]– True

Only 20% of cases present with the classic triad although dyspnoea and pleuritic chest pain occur in about 80%. 15% of cases have a normal ECG. Ventilation and perfusion scans are required to look for a mismatch between the two. Antithrombin III deficiency will be effectively excluded by a normal APTT before commencing treatment.

115 [A]– False [B]– True [C]– True [D]– True [E]– True

Prolactin is a stress hormone and less than 50% of women with a raised prolactin have galactorrhoea. The mechanism for renal failure-associated hyperprolactinaemia is not known.

116 A– True B– False C– False D– False E– True

Irritable bowel syndrome is a common disease in young
women and it is usually possible to diagnose this clinically
without the need to resort to laparoscopy, which carries a small
but very definite risk. Dyspareunia is common, as are other
functional symptoms such as menorrhagia and urinary
frequency.

117 A– True B– True C– True D– False E– True

Care must be taken in giving bromocriptine in the puerperium
as hypertensive episodes have occurred although more
commonly hypotension is the rule.

118 A– False B– True C– True D– True E– True

Ovarian remnant syndrome is where ovarian tissue can still be
demonstrated despite bilateral salpingo-oophorectomy.
Abolishing ovarian activity with GnRH analogues should
indicate whether the pain is ovarian or not and whether
surgery is required. The ureter must be identified and carefully
dissected from the ovary. Irritable bowel syndrome is still
common after hysterectomy but may have been present in the
first place as a cause of the symptoms for which the
hysterectomy was incorrectly performed.

119 [A]– False [B]– False [C]– **True** [D]– False [E]– False

Screening for ovarian cancer is still in the research stages but with two first degree relatives the offer of a prophylactic oophorectomy should be considered. If ultrasound screening is to be undertaken it must be done using Doppler and by someone with a special interest, as the number of patients with a strong family history is low and thus the number being screened per district low.

120 [A]– **True** [B]– False [C]– **True** [D]– False [E]– **True**

The CTG, fetal breathing, movements and tone and the depth of amniotic fluid constitute the biophysical profile. The suggestion from non controlled data was of great benefit from this form of assessment. Controlled studies, however, have not confirmed a better outcome for the baby from such tests and induction of labour is more effective in post dates pregnancies.

121 [A]– **True** [B]– False [C]– **True** [D]– **True** [E]– **True**

50% die by two months and 90% by one year. Choroid plexus cysts are an indication for detailed scanning as most should be identifiable at 20 weeks by the specific structural abnormalities, e.g. rocker bottom feet, characteristic skull appearance.

122 [A]– **True** [B]– **True** [C]– **True** [D]– **True** [E]– **True**

Bilateral salpingo-oophorectomy in all women over 40 will prevent only 8% of cases of ovarian cancer and such a policy would, on epidemiological data, lead to an increase in mortality from cardiovascular disease as compliance with HRT is so poor. Laparoscopic oophorectomy at the time of vaginal hysterectomy is useful as it is reasonably safe and avoids the potential ureteric damage of laparoscopic assisted vaginal hysterectomy which is commoner than standard vaginal hysterectomy.

123 A⊢ **True**　B⊢ False　C⊢ **True**　D⊢ **True**　E⊢ False

A high FSH indicates testicular failure and a biopsy can be useful to give information about spermatogenesis. Culture and microscopy for white blood cells is useful but testosterone has little value.

124 A⊢ False　B⊢ **True**　C⊢ False　D⊢ **True**　E⊢ **True**

Bromocriptine is a useful treatment, as is the contraceptive pill and danazol. There is an association with breast cancer due to the abnormal duct patterns and carcinoma in situ associated with mastalgia.

125 A⊢ False　B⊢ **True**　C⊢ False　D⊢ False　E⊢ **True**

Once the diagnosis has been made zoster immunoglobulin is of little use, but can be given to direct contacts including the child if born when the mother is infective. Acyclovir may be used if the woman is very ill, and this can happen in pregnancy, particularly due to pneumonia. The woman should avoid contact with other pregnant women.

126 A⊢ **True**　B⊢ False　C⊢ False　D⊢ **True**　E⊢ **True**

This patient requires immediate blood transfusion as she has lost at least one litre of blood. Induction should be instituted immediately by amniotomy and commencement of oxytocin and should not wait for the action of prostaglandins. Platelets are not indicated at this stage as they will be consumed in the coagulopathy, and the prime therapeutic manoeuvre is to empty the uterus. Post-partum haemorrhage is a problem, but mostly due to atony, not to coagulopathy.

127 A– False B– True C– True D– False E– True

Jaundice is not a specific complication of bottle feeding, but over-feeding is. It is difficult to over-feed a breastfed baby. Newborn tetany can occur due to the lower calcium phosphate ratio in cows' milk. Vitamin deficiencies do not occur as artificial feeds are supplemented with vitamins and iron. Diarrhoea is probably due to excess sugar or fat in bottle-fed babies as true cows' milk allergy is uncommon.

128 A– True B– True C– True D– True E– True

Hepatosplenomegaly may be normal but a massively enlarged spleen should be investigated. Congenital infection is a common cause, as are congenital abnormalities that lead to heart failure. Trisomy 18, thalassaemia and Rhesus incompatibility are all causes of hepatosplenomegaly.

129 A– True B– True C– True D– False E– True

Physiological jaundice does not start for about 24 hours and is commoner in breastfed babies. Sickle cell disease does not cause neonatal problems, but jaundice may be the only sign of a severe infection.

130 [A]– **True**   [B]– **True**   [C]– False   [D]– **True**   [E]– False

Blood sugar must be monitored carefully when tocolytics are in use, even in non-diabetics. Hypertension is a recognised problem and cardiac disease must be excluded before starting therapy. Pyrexia and renal faliure are not specific side-effects.

i 13339060